50 TRADITIONAL TOYS TO MAKE

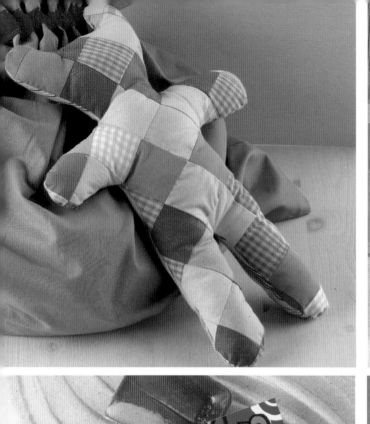

50 TRADITIONAL TOYS TO MAKE

Easy-to-follow projects to create for and with kids

Petra Boase

LORENZ BOOKS

This edition is published by Lorenz Books,
an imprint of Anness Publishing Ltd,
108 Great Russell Street,
London WC1B 3NA;
info@anness.com

www.lorenzbooks.com; www.annesspublishing.com

If you like the images in this book and would like
to investigate using them for publishing,
promotions or advertising, please visit our website
www.practicalpictures.com for more information.

Publisher: Joanna Lorenz
Senior Editor: Felicity Forster
Photography: James Duncan
Stylist: Petra Boase
Illustrator: Lucinda Ganderton
Designers: Lilian Lindblom and Lucy Doncaster
Production Controller: Pirong Wang

The author and publisher wish to thank
David and Jill Hancock for their contribution to this book.

Crafts and hobbies are great fun to learn and can fill hours of rewarding leisure time, but some points should be remembered for safety and care of the environment.
• Always choose non-toxic materials wherever possible – for example, paint, glue and varnish. Where these are not suitable, use materials in a well-ventilated area, and always follow the manufacturer's instructions.
• Craft knives, drills and all sharp tools should be handled with care. When sawing or drilling wood, make sure that the wood cannot slip.
• Protect surfaces with a cutting mat when using cutting tools, and with newspaper when using paint and glue.
• Make sure that any decorations you choose are suitable for the age of the child you are making the toy for. All decorations should be firmly attached.

CONTENTS

INTRODUCTION

Toys are a very important part of a child's growing years. Through playing with toys, so much is learnt and enjoyed.

The exciting projects in this book incorporate all kinds of materials and techniques. Many of them enable you to save odds and ends from around the home and recycle them. It is a useful idea to keep a cardboard box near the kitchen so you can store bottles, newspapers etc, until you are ready to use them.

Children can help make many of the projects, with supervision, but only adults should use saws, drills, knives and strong glue, and these should be stored in a safe place well out of children's reach.

The traditional toys in the following pages are guaranteed to delight children of all ages. There are wooden building blocks and a nursery mobile for babies; fun musical instruments and finger puppets for young kids; and absorbing games and outdoor toys for older children. Have fun creating some truly original playthings for your children!

Materials

Bottles
Only use plastic, rather than glass, bottles for the projects and save the tops for decoration. Please note, the tops are not suitable for decorating babies' toys.

Cardboard and paper
Cardboard and thin card (stock) come in a range of thicknesses. They sometimes needs to be cut with a craft (utility) knife rather than scissors. Newspaper is the core type of paper used for papier-mâché, and there is a huge range of other types of paper too.

Decorations
These are incredibly wide-ranging and the only limiting factor when choosing is making absolutely sure that the decoration you have selected for a toy is suitable for the age of the child you are making it for. Whichever you go for, all decorations should be very firmly attached. Choose from buttons (look in second-hand stores), furnishing fringing, bright pipe cleaners and pretty ribbons, including ribbon roses, adhesive shapes, or even shoelaces.

Fabrics
The choice of shades, patterns and textures is as wide as you could wish for. You may prefer to choose natural ones, such as cotton and linen, for children. Felt is soft and has the added advantage of being easy to cut without fraying. It is also available with an adhesive backing that means it can easily be used to cover objects.

Fasteners
Paper fasteners can be used to join two pieces of cardboard or paper together, while still allowing them to move. Poppers (snap fasteners) or press studs are used for fastening fabric. Self-adhesive fabric tape is a quick and easy fastener for fabric.

Glues and tapes
Double-sided tape can be used instead of glue to stick paper or cardboard. Electrical tape is very strong and can be used to join heavy materials. It can also be used for decoration and it comes in a range of shades. Masking tape is useful for reinforcing cardboard shapes and for marking out areas before painting. PVA (white) glue is a water-based, non-toxic glue and is ideal for sticking wood or paper. It can also be diluted with water and used in papier-mâché or as a quick varnish.

Paints
Water-based paints are non-toxic and ideal for babies' and children's toys. Choose from either poster, acrylic or emulsion (latex) paints. Enamel paints are oil-based paints that will adhere to metal, wood or plastic. Spray paints are mostly toxic when wet, so use them outdoors or in a well-ventilated room and always wear a mask.

Polymer clay
This is a modelling medium that is available in a range of shades. Follow the manufacturer's instructions, as products do vary.

Safety pin
Use this to help thread ribbon or cord through a fabric tube.

Screw eyes
These are screwed into the back of a piece of wood (for example, a picture frame) so that cord can be threaded through them and the item can be hung.

Stuffing
This is used to fill toys and shapes made from fabric and is more malleable than wadding (batting).

Ties
Cord is stronger than either string or ribbon and can be threaded through a drawstring bag to pull it shut and for carrying. Rope is stronger still, although nylon rope does tend to unravel at the ends unless you seal them by burning them (see Techniques).

Threads and needles
Embroidery threads (floss) are used in hand-sewing to make bright, detailed stitches. For ordinary hand- or machine-sewing choose either cotton or rayon thread. Choose an appropriately sized needle for the thickness of the thread.

Wood
Balsa wood is a very soft wood that can be bought from model stores. MDF (medium-density fiberboard) is a man-made wood and is much stronger than balsa wood. Wear a mask when sawing as it produces a fine dust.

self-adhesive fabric spots

fabric

matchsticks

strong glue

bright paper

cork

newspaper

safety pins

adhesive stars

cord

rope

paper fasteners

balsa wood

MDF (medium-density fiberboard)

electrical tape

masking tape

double-sided tape

screw eyes

spray paint

enamel paints

paper bauble

felt

stuffing

bottle top

varnish

buttons

cotton thread

paints

pipe cleaners

ribbon roses

poppers (snap fasteners)

zip (zipper)

squeaker

dowel

paper fasteners

ribbon

polymer clay

plastic bottle

embroidery threads (floss)

PVA (white) glue

shoelaces

cardboard

fringing

Equipment

Abrasive paper
Use this to sand the edges and surfaces of pieces of wood smooth before they are painted.

Bradawl or awl
This is a tool with a sharp point that is used for making holes in wood or cardboard.

Craft (utility) knife
More accurate than scissors, a craft knife can be used in conjunction with a metal ruler to cut cardboard. Protect your work surface with a sheet of thick cardboard or a use a special cutting mat. Keep all knives out of the reach of children.

Coping saw
This is a special saw with a flexible blade for cutting out awkward shapes of wood. Take great care when using a saw and make sure all children are well out of the way before you start working. Store in a safe place.

Dressmaking pins and needles
Pins are useful for holding pieces of fabric together before you stitch them in place. There are many types of needle, from ones with small eyes for cotton thread to tapestry needles with large heads and blunt points. Choose one that is suitable for the thread and the fabric you are using.

Drills and drill bits
These are used to drill holes in pieces of wood and other materials. Drill bits come in a range of sizes.

Fretsaw
This is used to cut small, intricate shapes in wood and plastic. The blade can be removed and inserted in a guide hole, then the saw reassembled to allow you to make cut-out shapes in a piece of wood. Keep children well out of range when using one and store safely out of their reach.

Hole punch
Use this to make neat holes in paper and thin card (stock). They are available in a range of sizes.

Iron
This is very useful for patchwork to press open the seams.

Modelling tools
These are used to shape and make impressions in polymer clay, non-hardening modelling clay and other modelling mediums.

Paintbrushes
Available in a wide range of different sizes – and prices, depending on quality. Keep them in good condition by washing them immediately after use, so the paint doesn't harden.

Pair of compasses
Use these for drawing accurate circles. Alternatively, draw around a cup, saucer, plate or other circular household object.

Pastry cutters
These are excellent for cutting out shapes from polymer clay and other modelling mediums.

Pencils
These can be used for drawing and for tracing templates.

Pinking shears
These useful scissors cut with a decorative zigzag line and prevent fabric edges from fraying.

Pliers
These are used for cutting and bending wire.

Rolling pin
Use one to roll out polymer clay and other modelling mediums. Keep it solely for craft use and don't use it again in the kitchen.

Scissors
These come in a variety of sizes and it is best to have one pair for cutting paper and another for fabric, as cutting paper would blunt fabric scissors, which need to be very sharp.

Screwdrivers
As the name suggests, these are used for driving screws into pieces of wood or other materials. There are two main types of tip – cross-head and blade – and they each work with certain types of screw. It is useful to have several of each kind in different sizes.

Tenon saw
Use a tenon saw to cut large or thick pieces of wood. Take great care when using a saw, and make sure all children are well out of the way when you are working. Store safely out of reach.

scissors

paintbrushes

modelling tools

pencil

pliers

rolling pin

abrasive paper

coping saw

pair of compasses

pastry cutter

bradawl or awl

dressmaker's pins

craft (utility) knife

drill piece

single-hole punch

tapestry needle

knitting needles

fretsaw

pinking shears

tenon saw

screwdriver

TECHNIQUES

Papier-mâché

Papier-mâché is a great way to make something creative and recycle newspapers at the same time.

YOU WILL NEED
newspaper
PVA (white) glue and brush
bowl
water
abrasive paper
paintbrush
white emulsion (latex) paint
acrylic paints
varnish and brush

1 Tear up sheets of newspaper into small squares.

2 Pour some PVA glue into a bowl and slowly add water, mixing at the same time to make a smooth paste.

3 Glue the newspaper evenly over a shape or mould and gradually build up layers. Leave the papier-mâché in a warm, dry place to dry overnight, or until it is hard.

4 Lightly rub the dried papier-mâché with some abrasive paper to smooth the surface.

5 Paint the papier-mâché with a white undercoat of emulsion paint. When the undercoat is dry, paint on the acrylic paints.

6 When the paint has dried, apply a coat of varnish. Leave to dry.

Sanding wood

It is very important to smooth the surface and corners of wood before painting as this will avoid splintering.

Use abrasive paper to smooth any rough edges on sawn wood.

Drilling wood

When drilling through wood, make sure you protect your work surface adequately. Adults only should use a drill.

Place an old piece of wood under the piece you want to drill.

Sealing rope ends

Some of the projects use rope and adults only will need to seal the ends to prevent them unravelling.

Carefully burn the rope ends and then put them outside on a stone or concrete surface to cool. Do not let children do this.

Stuffing soft toys

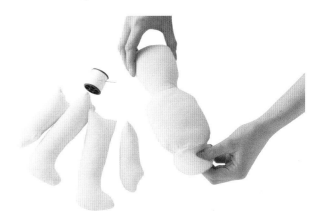

Push stuffing to the ends of toy pieces, using a knitting needle or the end of a wooden spoon to reach small or awkward shapes.

Stitches

Several of the needlework projects use decorative stitches, some of which you may be familiar with.

French knots

1 Tie a knot at the end of the sewing thread, then stitch through to the right side of the fabric. Using a needle, make a knot close to the fabric. Adult supervision is required.

2 Pass the needle back through the fabric again close to the knot.

Blanket stitch

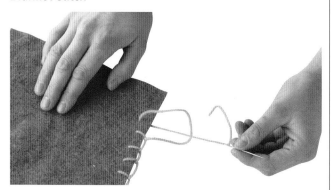

Use this stitch for edging fabric to prevent it from fraying. Tie a knot at the end of the sewing thread or wool (yarn), and pass it through the fabric from the wrong side. Push the needle through the right side of the fabric 1cm (½in) farther on and place the needle over the loop to form a stitch. Repeat.

Bending wire

1 Use a pair of pliers to help you bend a piece of wire into shape. Adult supervision is required.

2 To secure the two ends of the wire together, twist them and press hard with the tips of the pliers.

Making a hole in a can

Place a ball of softened non-hardening modelling clay on the can where you want to make a hole (this will prevent the bradawl or awl from slipping), then pierce it with a bradawl or awl. Adults only should do this.

Tracing templates

Some of the projects in this book include templates that you can trace. These instructions show you how to transfer a template to another piece of paper if you don't have access to a photocopier.

Scaling up

Some of the templates in the book are smaller than the size you need for the project, so you will need to scale them up. If you have access to a computer or photocopier, you can use it to enlarge the shapes. Otherwise, follow these instructions.

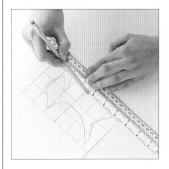

1 Place a piece of tracing paper over the required template in the book and draw over the shape with a pencil.

2 Remove the tracing paper and turn it over. Rub over the traced image with a pencil on the reverse side of the tracing paper.

1 Draw a rectangle or square to the nearest 2.5cm (1in) around the image you want to enlarge. Divide it into 2.5cm (1in) squares.

2 On a separate piece of paper, draw another box as large as you want but in proportion to the first box. Divide it into even squares.

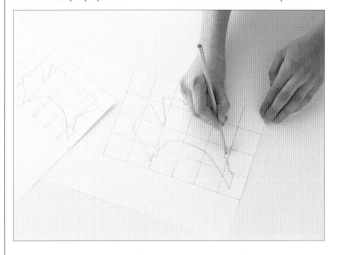

3 Place the tracing paper on top of a piece of thin card (stock) or paper, with the rubbed pencil side facing down. Draw over the shape again, pressing firmly with the pencil, to transfer the image.

4 Cut out the shape. You now have a template to draw around. You can use it on paper, card or fabric.

3 Copy the image in the large box, using the squares to help you. Trace the image to make the template.

TEMPLATES

Some of the projects in this book require templates. You can either trace the templates and scale them up to the size required following the instructions given earlier, or scan them and use a computer or printer to increase their size.

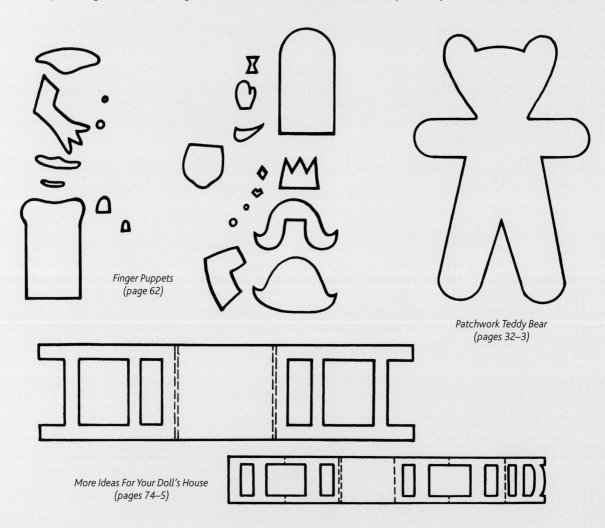

Finger Puppets
(page 62)

Patchwork Teddy Bear
(pages 32–3)

More Ideas For Your Doll's House
(pages 74–5)

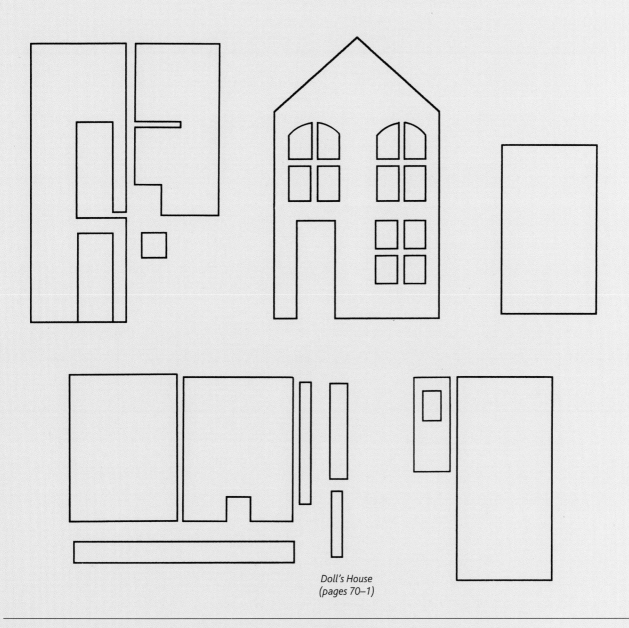

Doll's House
(pages 70–1)

Flower Power Cushion
(pages 26–7)

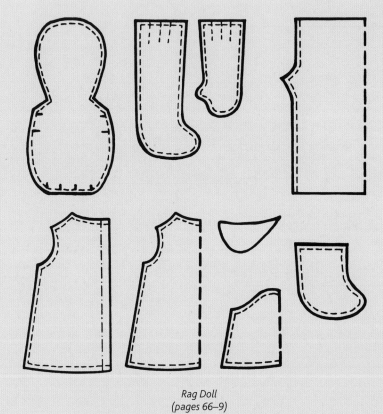

Rag Doll
(pages 66–9)

Glove Puppets
(page 63)

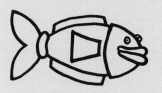

Magnetic Fish
(page 87)

Dog Jigsaw
(page 52)

Dog and Bone Mobile
(pages 34–5)

Felt Picture Book
(page 45)

Paper Fastener Puppet
(page 64)

Felt Noughts and Crosses (Tic-tac-toe)
(pages 82–3)

Toy Bag
(page 25)

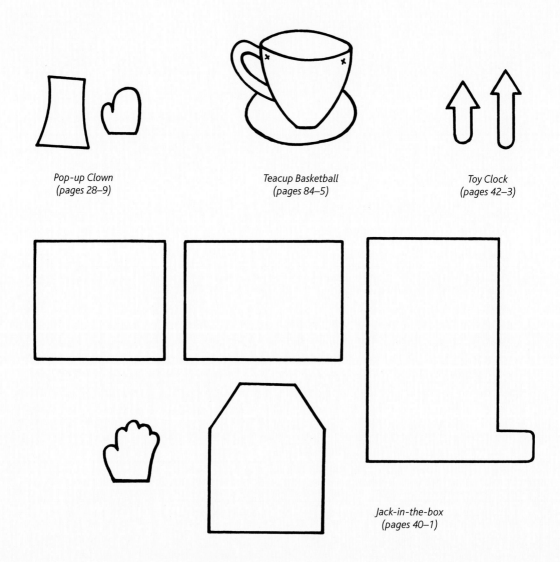

Pop-up Clown
(pages 28–9)

Teacup Basketball
(pages 84–5)

Toy Clock
(pages 42–3)

Jack-in-the-box
(pages 40–1)

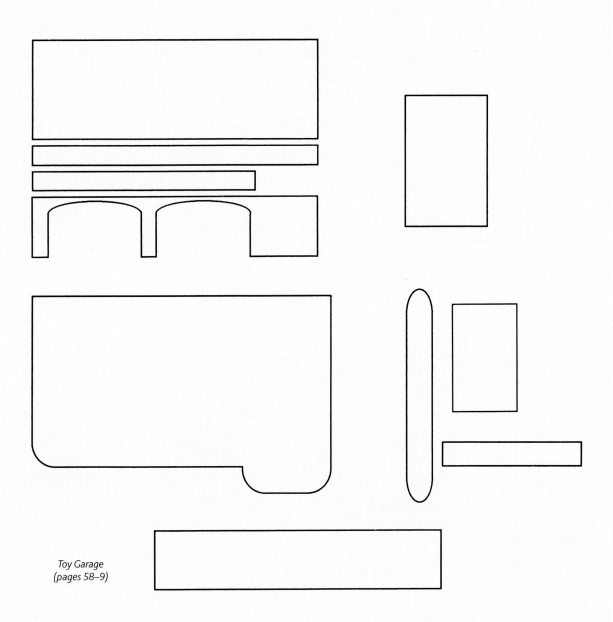

Toy Garage
(pages 58–9)

Squeaky Square

This soft, cuddly toy has a surprise squeaker tucked inside it. You can purchase a squeaker from craft and haberdashery (notions) stores. Using odds and ends of knitting wool (yarn) in bright cheerful shades, this simple toy can be made by most knitters who know the basics.

YOU WILL NEED
knitting wool (yarn),
  in assorted shades
knitting needles
tapestry needle
stuffing
squeaker

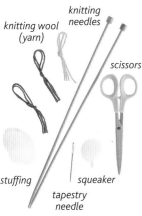

knitting wool (yarn)

knitting needles

scissors

stuffing

squeaker

tapestry needle

1 For each triangle, cast on 11 stitches. Knit every row, decreasing 1 stitch on every second row, until you are left with 2 stitches. Cast off. Make eight triangles in total in different shades.

2 For the large middle square, cast on 20 stitches. Knit in stocking stitch until you have about 24 rows, or a square. Make two squares in total in the same way and in the same shade.

3 Using matching wool and a tapestry needle, stitch the two squares together, trapping the triangles around the edge. Leave out one triangle so that there is a gap for the stuffing.

4 Fill the cavity between the two knitted squares with the stuffing.

5 Place the squeaker in the middle of the stuffing.

6 Insert the remaining triangle and stitch up the opening securely using small stitches, ensuring no stuffing can escape.

Decoupage Toy Box

Jazz up a toy box with paint and some cut-outs. Children will love selecting the pictures to be cut out and helping to glue them on to the box. A layer of varnish means the shapes will not rub off and the finished decoration is hardwearing.

YOU WILL NEED
wooden toy box
abrasive paper
emulsion (latex) paint,
  in several shades
paintbrush
wrapping paper
scissors
PVA (white) glue and brush
varnish and brush

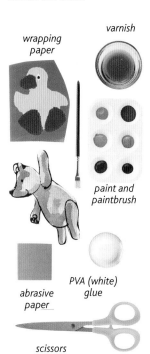

wrapping paper

varnish

paint and paintbrush

PVA (white) glue

abrasive paper

scissors

1 First sand down the toy box with abrasive paper. Paint the box with emulsion paint, using a different shade for each side. Leave the paint to dry completely, then apply a second coat.

2 When the paint is dry, cut out shapes from the wrapping paper. Children should be supervised when using scissors.

3 Arrange the paper shapes on the box to make a good design. Using the PVA glue, paste them in place.

4 When the glue is dry, varnish the box, leave it to dry completely and fill it with toys!

Toy Bag

This bag can be made by adults or older children, with supervision. It can be used to store toys at home or if you are going out for the day. Position the star so that it will be in the middle of one side of the bag when the fabric is folded in half.

YOU WILL NEED
paper
pencil
scissors
scraps of fabric, for the star
fabric glue and brush
dressmaker's needle and
    matching sewing threads
52 x 110cm (20½ x 43in)
    hardwearing fabric
1m (39in) bright tape
1.5m (59in) ribbon or cord
safety pin

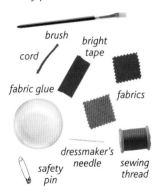

brush
bright tape
cord
fabric glue
fabrics
dressmaker's needle
safety pin
sewing thread

1 Trace the star shape from the template at the front of the book on to paper. Place this on the reverse side of a scrap of fabric and cut it out. Cut out spots in a contrasting shades and glue them on to the right side of the star. Stitch the star on to the right side of the bag fabric.

2 With right sides facing, fold the fabric in half to make a square. Stitch along the sides, leaving a 1cm (½in) seam allowance.

3 Fold over the open side by 5cm (2in), then stitch around the top. Turn right side out. Starting at a side seam, pin the tape around the outside of the bag 3cm (1¼in) from the top.

4 Fold in the raw ends, then stitch along either side of the tape. Attach a safety pin to the end of the ribbon or cord and thread it through the tube. Tie the ends in a knot.

Flower Power Cushion

This patchwork cushion is decorated with sunny flowers, just right for small fingers to hold on to. The flowers are attached with self-adhesive fabric tape so you can move them about. Older children can make this project, with supervision.

YOU WILL NEED
tracing paper
paper
pencil
scissors
scraps of felt in assorted shades,
    for the flowers
embroidery threads (floss),
    in assorted shades
embroidery needle
16cm (6½in) self-adhesive
    fabric tape
4 pieces of felt, each 22cm
    (8½in) square, in different
    shades
sewing thread and needle
stuffing
dressmaker's pins
2 pieces of fabric, each 40 x 30cm
    (16 x 12in), for the cushion back
40cm (16in) square cushion pad
zip fastener (zipper), optional

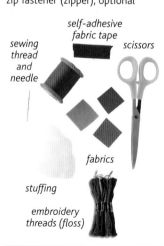

self-adhesive fabric tape
sewing thread and needle
scissors
fabrics
stuffing
embroidery threads (floss)

1 Trace the flower shape from the template. Draw around it four times on felt in various shades. Cut out four circles for the flower middles in contrast shades, and embroider with French knots.

2 Cut the self-adhesive fabric tape into four equal pieces. Stitch one half of each piece to the back of each flower, and stitch the other half to the middle of one of the felt squares.

3 Position the flower middles on top of the flowers, trapping a small ball of stuffing in between the layers. Pin in place with dressmaker's pins, then neatly stitch around the flower middles.

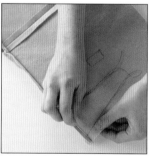

4 For the patchwork, place two of the felt squares together. Hand- or machine-stitch, leaving a 1cm (½in) seam allowance. Join the other two squares the same way, then stitch the two sets of squares together to make a large block.

5 Place the two pieces of fabric for the cushion back on the felt block, right sides together. Pin, then stitch around all four sides, leaving a 1cm (½in) seam allowance. Fold back the raw edges of the back pieces and attach in the seam.

6 Turn the cushion cover right side out and insert the cushion pad. Stitch the opening using slip stitch or insert a zip fastener if you want to be able to remove the cushion. Stick the flowers on to the front using the self-adhesive fabric strips.

Pop-up Clown

All you need to make this toy is a piece of dowel and scraps of fabric, felt and trimmings. Children can help paint the features and choose the fabrics used, and older children can assemble the clown, too.

YOU WILL NEED
35cm (13¾in) dowel
craft (utility) knife
small paper ball
emulsion (latex) paint, in red
  and another shade
paintbrush
pencil
thin card (stock)
scissors
masking tape
felt, in pink and two
  other shades
fabric glue
paper
sewing needle and matching
  sewing threads
scraps of fabric
lampshade trimming
Ric-rac
12cm (4¾in) ribbon
small pompom

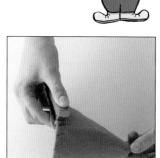

1 Carefully sharpen one end of the dowel into a point using a craft knife, then push the sharpened end into the paper ball so it is secure. An adult must do this. Paint the dowel rod and leave it to dry. Meanwhile, paint a clown's face on the paper ball and leave it to dry.

2 Draw an 8cm- (3in-) radius semi-circle on to thin card. Cut out the circle, bend it into a cone shape and secure with masking tape. Cut a slightly larger piece of felt and glue this on to the cone, folding the edges to the inside. Trace the hand and sleeve templates.

3 For each hand, fold a piece of pink felt in half, place the template on top and draw around it. Stitch along the marked line, then cut out, adding a 3mm (⅛in) seam allowance. Turn right side out. For the sleeves, fold a piece of fabric in half, right sides together. Continue as for the hands.

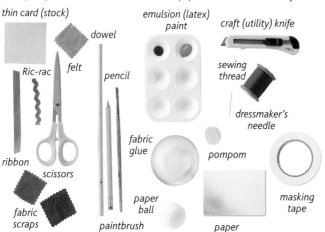

thin card (stock)

dowel

Ric-rac *felt*

pencil

ribbon

scissors

fabric scraps

fabric glue

paintbrush

paper ball

emulsion (latex) paint

craft (utility) knife

sewing thread

dressmaker's needle

pompom

paper

masking tape

4 Tuck the hands in the sleeve openings and stitch. For the shirt, cut two pieces of fabric 14 x 8cm (5½ x 3in) and place right sides together. Insert the arms at an angle on either side. Stitch the side seams, then turn right side out. Hem the top edge.

5 Glue the bottom edge of the shirt to the top of the cone and leave to dry. Glue a piece of lampshade trimming around the top of the cone, neatly covering the raw edges. Decorate the trimming with a strip of Ric-rac. Leave the glue to dry completely.

6 Push the dowel rod through the card cone. Stitch around the top of the shirt in running stitch and pull up the thread to make gathers. Glue to the rod just below the clown's head. Gather the ribbon the same way, stitching along one edge, to make a ruff and glue around the clown's neck. Draw a 4cm (1½in) radius semi-circle on to card, cut out, then cut out of felt. Fold in half and stitch the seam to make the hat. Turn right side out and stitch on a pompom. Decorate the bottom of the hat with Ric-rac.

Knitted Cot Toy

Babies love to reach out and grasp these soft, squidgy shapes hanging in a line across a cot or crib. The squares and triangles are easy to make, and the project is suitable for older children who are learning to knit. You could add some beads if you like.

YOU WILL NEED
knitting wool (yarn),
    in assorted shades
knitting needles
tapestry needle
stuffing
cord
scissors

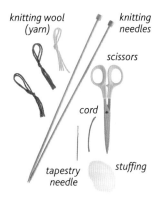

knitting wool
(yarn)

knitting
needles

scissors

cord

tapestry
needle

stuffing

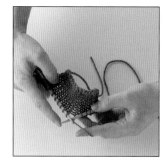

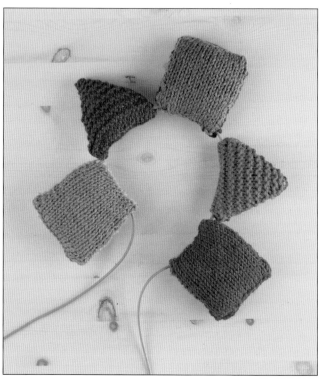

1 For each square, cast on 15 stitches and knit 21 rows in stocking stitch. Cast off. Knit six squares in three different shades. For each triangle, cast on 20 stitches and knit in stocking stitch, decreasing 1 stitch every second row until you are left with 2 stitches. Cast off. Knit four triangles in two different shades. Using matching wool, stitch the pairs of shapes together, leaving one side open for stuffing.

2 Fill all the shapes with stuffing.

3 Using wool that matches the shade of one of the knitted squares, sew up the openings securely using small stitches, making sure the stuffing can't escape.

4 Using the tapestry needle, thread the cord through one side of each square and through the straight edge of the triangles. Knot the cord between the shapes.

Knitted Polar Bear

The body of this polar bear is knitted in garter stitch and is all in one piece, making it simple to put together.

YOU WILL NEED
50g (2oz) white or cream Aran, knitting wool (yarn)
4.5mm (size 7) knitting needles
scissors
tapestry needle
black knitting or tapestry wool (yarn)
stuffing

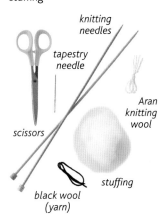

knitting needles
tapestry needle
Aran knitting wool
scissors
stuffing
black wool (yarn)

1 Cast on 40 stitches and knit for 20 rows. Cast off 10 stitches at each end of the next row (20 stitches). Knit 18 rows, then cast on 10 stitches at each end of the next row (40 stitches). Knit 20 rows. Cast off 10 stitches at each end of the next row (20 stitches). Knit 2 rows. Cast off 1 stitch at the end of every second row until you have only 2 stitches. Cast off.

2 Stitch up the hind legs and bottom seam as far as the stomach. Leave a gap for the stuffing. Stitch the nose in black wool. Stitch the front legs. Stuff the bear, then stitch the gap.

3 To make the bear's ears, pinch a small piece of knitting either side of the face, making sure they are equal in size. Wrap a piece of wool around each ear and stitch.

4 Stitch the eyes and mouth in black wool.

Patchwork Teddy Bear

Stitch the patches used to make this bear securely together by hand or using a sewing machine so that the stuffing can't come out. Adult supervision is required if older children make this toy. Younger children can help choose the pieces of fabric.

YOU WILL NEED
cardboard
ruler
pencil
paper
scissors
assorted fabrics
needle and sewing threads
iron
dressmaker's pins
fabric pen or tailor's chalk
stuffing

scissors

stuffing

dressmaker's needle

fabric pen

fabrics

dressmaker's pins

sewing thread

cardboard

pencil

ruler

1 Draw a 6cm (2½in) square on cardboard and cut it out. Place the cardboard on the reverse side of the fabrics and cut out squares. You will need about 80 squares altogether, all the same size and in lots of different shades.

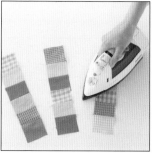

2 With right sides facing, stitch two squares together along one side, leaving a 5mm (³/₁₆in) seam allowance. Stitch pairs of squares together to make strips. Press the seams with an iron so they lie in one direction.

3 Trace the teddy bear shape from the template at the front of the book and enlarge it on to cardboard or paper to 36cm (14in) long. Stitch the strips together to make a piece of patchwork large enough to fit the template.

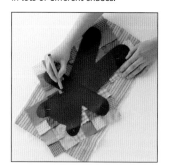

4 Cut a piece of fabric the same size as the patchwork for the back of the teddy. Pin the two together, right sides facing. Draw around the bear template with a fabric pen or tailor's chalk.

5 Hand- or machine-stitch around the shape, leaving a 5cm (2in) opening for the stuffing. Cut out the teddy bear, leaving a 1cm (½in) border. Then turn right side out and fill with stuffing.

6 Slip-stitch the opening securely, using small stitches and making sure that no stuffing can escape.

Dog and Bone Mobile

This witty mobile is great fun to make with and for children, although adults only must use the saw, drill and knife. Trace the shapes from the templates supplied, cut them out of card and ask children to paint them in bright shades. Hang the rods up before tying on the shapes, as it will be easier to balance them at this stage.

YOU WILL NEED
2 x 45cm (18in) pieces of dowel,
  5mm (³⁄₁₆in) diameter
saw
abrasive paper
drill and drill bit
craft (utility) knife
poster paint, in assorted shades
paintbrush
cord
adhesive tape, optional
tracing paper
pencil
thin card (stock)
scissors
single-hole punch
thread, in assorted shades

pencil

single-hole punch   dowel

abrasive paper

scissors

poster paint

drill and drill bit

saw

paintbrush

threads

craft (utility) knife

1 Cut the dowel to size and smooth the ends with abrasive paper. Drill a hole in the middle of each dowel.

4 Trace the mobile shapes from the templates at the front of the book and transfer them to thin card. Cut out the shapes. Punch a hole on each shape where marked on the templates. Older children can help with this, with supervision.

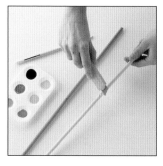

2 Using a craft knife, shave a 'V' shape around the hole on one of the rods. This will help the rods to sit comfortably at right angles to each other. Paint each rod using a different shade and leave to dry.

5 Ask a child to paint the shapes on both sides, using bright shades, or do it yourself. Leave the paint to dry completely.

3 Thread a piece of cord through the holes and tie in a knot either side of the dowel rods. If you have trouble threading the cord through the holes, wrap a piece of adhesive tape tightly around the end first.

6 Tie on the shapes to the dowel rods, spacing them so the shapes hang nicely, using a thread in a different shade for each.

Basic Jigsaw

This simple jigsaw is a good one to have a go with before moving on to making ones with more pieces. It makes an ideal present for a young child, especially if you paint a bright design on the pieces.

YOU WILL NEED
30cm (12in) square of cardboard
pencil
paint, in bright shades
paintbrush
craft (utility) knife

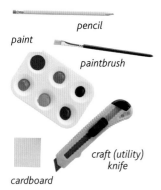

pencil

paint

paintbrush

craft (utility) knife

cardboard

1 Draw a picture on the cardboard, using a pencil, or ask a child to draw a picture.

2 Ask a child to paint the picture, using bright shades, or do it yourself. Leave the paint to dry.

3 Turn the cardboard over and divide the square into four even-sized sections. Draw a simple jigsaw shape on each section.

4 Carefully cut along the drawn lines, using a craft knife, to create the four pieces of the puzzle. An adult should do this.

Wire Mobile

These painted wire shapes make an attractive mobile and are easy to make for a simple but stylish gift. Farmyard animals are the theme here, but you could ask a child to create their own design, such as dinosaurs or fish.

YOU WILL NEED
galvanized steel wire
pliers
enamel paint, in assorted shades
paintbrush
threads, in assorted shades
turpentine

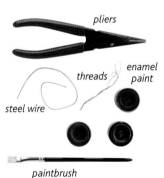

pliers

threads   enamel paint

steel wire

paintbrush

1 Bend the wire into the shapes you want with the help of a pair of pliers. When you have completed a shape, twist the two ends of the wire firmly together, ensuring they will not come undone.

2 Paint each animal shape with different enamel paints and hang them up from a piece of thread to dry. Wash the paintbrushes with turpentine immediately after you have finished painting to remove all traces of the paint.

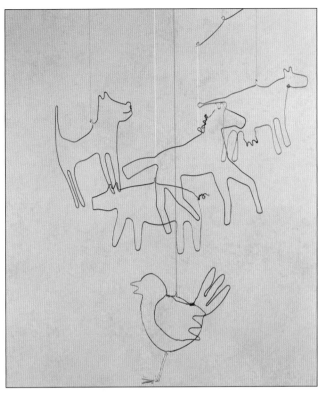

3 Cut three pieces of wire 20cm (8in) long. Bend each piece to make a loop in the middle and a loop at either end of the wire.

4 Lay the three pieces of wire on a flat surface and position the shapes around them. Tie the shapes to the loops with bright threads.

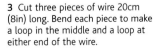

Wooden Boat

Children of all ages will enjoy imaginary journeys in this ocean-liner, and can help paint it (but not saw or drill). Built in pine, it is too heavy to float but is ideal to play with on land.

YOU WILL NEED
saw
43cm (17in) of 8 x 5cm
  (3 x 2in) pine
16cm (6½in) of 8mm
  (⅝in) dowel
abrasive paper
pencil
drill, with 8mm (⅝in) drill bit
wood glue
acrylic paint: pale blue,
  turquoise, navy, red, white
  and gold
paintbrush
varnish and brush

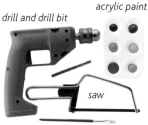

drill and drill bit   *acrylic paint*

saw

paintbrush
          wood glue
pine

dowel

abrasive paper   *varnish*

pencil

1 Saw the pine into two lengths, 17cm (6¾in) and 26cm (10½in), and cut the dowel into four equal lengths. Sand with abrasive paper until smooth.

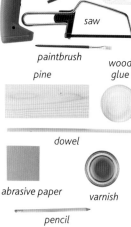

4 Mark out with pencil and then saw a pointed bow shape on one end of the large piece of pine, to make the base of the boat. Sand the surface with abrasive paper until smooth, then glue the shorter piece of pine that you have fixed the funnels into on top, as shown in the photograph above.

2 For the portholes, draw a line on the shorter piece of pine along each of the 8cm (3in) sides, 2.5cm (1in) from the top. Starting at one end, mark with a pencil 3cm (1½in), 5cm (2in), 7cm (2¾in) and so on until you reach 13cm (5in). Drill into the pine at these points.

5 Paint the boat, following the design shown in the photograph as a guide or making up your own design. If you want to paint a name on the bows of the boat, do it at this stage.

3 For the funnels of the boat, mark a line down the middle of one of the 5cm- (2in-) wide sides of the same piece of pine. Mark points at 3.5cm (1¾in), 7cm (2¾in), 10.5cm (4¼in) and 14cm (5½in). Drill shallow holes at these points and glue in the lengths of dowel using wood glue.

6 When the paint is dry, apply a coat of varnish and then leave it to dry completely.

Jack-in-the-box

Lift the lid of this magician's box for a real surprise! The jolly clown inside is easy to make, using odds and ends of fabric and paper. Children can help with the painting.

YOU WILL NEED

FOR THE BOX
6mm (¼in) birch plywood sheet
saw
ruler
abrasive paper
wood glue and brush
masking tape
brass hinge
undercoat
paintbrush
acrylic paint: blue and gold
varnish and brush

FOR THE CLOWN
tracing paper
pencil
paper
scissors
scraps of fabric
felt
fabric glue
white paper balls
crayons

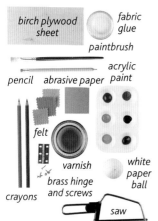

birch plywood sheet

fabric glue

paintbrush

acrylic paint

pencil   abrasive paper

felt

varnish

white paper ball

brass hinge and screws

crayons

saw

1 Following the template, cut out all the pieces for the box. Smooth the surfaces and corners thoroughly with abrasive paper. Glue the box together, except for the lid. Hold the pieces in place with masking tape until the glue dries.

2 Attach the lid to the box with the hinge, making sure that the lid closes square to the box. Paint the outside of the box and both sides of the lid with undercoat. A child can help with this; cover the work surface with newspaper. Leave to dry.

3 Paint the box and both sides of the lid with blue acrylic paint. When this is completely dry, paint on gold stars. Again, a child could help with this, with supervision. When the paint is completely dry, varnish the box and lid.

4 Trace the shapes for the clown's clothes from the templates at the front of the book. Cut the shapes out of fabric. Cut out the hands, diamond-shaped buttons and a sawtooth-edge collar and stick on the clothes with fabric glue.

5 Draw a simple clown face on one side of the ball of paper and decorate it with bright crayons. A child would enjoy doing this. Cut a triangle of felt and glue it around the head above the face to make a hat, as shown in the final photograph.

6 Put some glue on the back of the collar and stick it to the bottom half of the open lid. Apply lots of glue to the back of the hat and glue it to the lid directly above the glued collar. Leave the glue to dry completely before using the toy.

Toy Clock

Recycle your breakfast cereal packet to make a friendly clock, as a fun way of learning how to tell the time. An older child can do most of the tasks in this project, with adult supervision, apart from piercing the hole in the cardboard.

YOU WILL NEED
cardboard
pencil
scissors
emulsion (latex) paint,
  in assorted shades
paintbrush
craft (utility) knife
paper fastener
cereal box
adhesive plastic: blue and yellow
double-sided tape

adhesive plastic

paper fastener

scissors

emulsion (latex) paints

paintbrush

cardboard

double-sided tape

craft (utility) knife

pencil

1 Draw around a small plate on to cardboard and cut it out. Find the middle of the circle and pierce a hole with the scissors. An adult should pierce the hole.

2 Paint the circle in a bright shade and leave it to dry completely. Paint the numerals in the appropriate positions around the clock face in contrasting shades and leave to dry.

3 Trace the clock hands from the template at the front of the book on to cardboard and cut them out. Paint and attach the arms to the clock with a paper fastener.

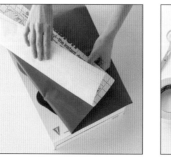

4 Cover the cereal box with blue adhesive plastic and smooth it down, trying to avoid air bubbles. If necessary, run a ruler over the plastic to eliminate any little bubbles.

5 Stick the clock face on to the box with double-sided tape. Cut out stars from yellow adhesive plastic and stick these on to the sides of the box.

6 Stick more stars on the front of the clock around the face. Stand up the clock and use it to teach children to tell the time.

Activity Blanket

Tiny fingers will love playing with this blanket, and at the same time they will learn how to use zips (zippers), buttons and shoelaces. Make sure all the pieces are securely attached, especially the buttons.

YOU WILL NEED
bright blanket
tapestry wool (yarn),
  in bright shades
tapestry needle
scissors
bright zips (zippers)
dressmaker's pins
scraps of blanket or felt in
  contrasting shades
buttons
pompoms
laces

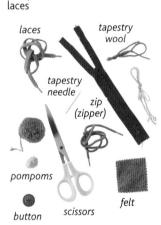

laces · tapestry wool · tapestry needle · zip (zipper) · pompoms · scissors · felt · button

1 Cut the blanket to the size you want, if necessary. Fold under the edges and blanket-stitch in place, using contrasting tapestry wool. An older child with some experience of sewing may be able to do this with adult supervision.

2 Position the zips on the blanket and pin in place. Secure with running stitch, using contrasting tapestry wool.

3 Cut out simple shapes, such as squares, circles and triangles, from blanket or felt. Cut a slit in the middle of each shape for a button to go through. Stitch the buttons on to the blanket and fasten on the shapes to the buttons.

4 Sew on pompoms and laces as more shapes to play with. If an older child has done the sewing, an adult should double-check that all the elements are securely sewn in position and cannot easily be pulled off.

Felt Picture Book

The great thing about this eye-catching book is that you don't have to worry about the pages getting torn or crumpled. An older child could make this themselves, with supervision, and younger children can help with gluing.

YOU WILL NEED
paper
pencil
scissors
scraps of felt, for the pictures
5 pieces of felt, 6cm (2½in) square, in different shades
fabric glue and brush
6.5cm (2¾in) strip of felt, for the spine
embroidery thread (floss)
embroidery needle

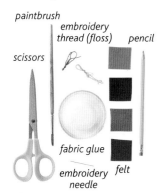

paintbrush
embroidery thread (floss)
pencil
scissors
fabric glue
embroidery needle
felt

1 Trace the shapes from the templates at the front of the book on to paper and cut out. Lay the paper shapes on scraps of felt in different shades and cut out.

2 Position the felt shapes on the felt squares to make the pictures. Glue the different pieces in place. Leave the glue to dry completely.

3 Place the felt squares on top of each other, with the pictures facing upwards. Place a plain felt square on top. Cut the felt spine to the length of the book, fold in half and glue around the edge, trapping all the pages inside. Leave to dry.

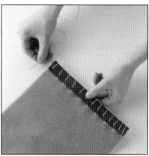

4 To secure the spine, stitch through all the layers with embroidery thread, using a contrasting shade and neat blanket stitch for a smart, robust finish.

Bottle Maracas

*Hold one of these in each hand and shake them in time to
music. For instructions on how to cover the bottles with
papier-mâché, see the Techniques section at the beginning
of the book. A child can help with this project.*

YOU WILL NEED

FOR THE PAPIER-MÂCHÉ
newspaper
bowl
water
PVA (white) glue and brush

FOR THE MARACAS
2 small, empty plastic bottles
emulsion (latex) paint, in
   assorted shades
paintbrush
buttons
strong glue
A4 (11¾ x 8½in) sheet of paper
100g (4oz) lentils or other dried
   pulses (legumes)
2 pieces of balsa wood, each
   12cm (4¾in) long
craft (utility) knife
bright electrical tape

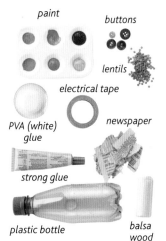

paint

buttons

lentils

electrical tape

*PVA (white)
glue*

newspaper

strong glue

plastic bottle

*balsa
wood*

1 Make sure the bottles are clean
and dry. Cover both bottles with
two layers of papier-mâché.

2 When the papier-mâché is dry,
paint the bottles all over in a base
shade. Leave to dry.

3 Paint bright patterns on top of
the base paint. Leave the paint to
dry completely.

4 Glue buttons around the bottom
of the bottles with strong glue.
Adults must do this stage – do not
let children use strong glue. Leave
to dry.

5 Roll the sheet of paper into a cone and fit it into the top of one of the bottles.
Pour half the lentils or pulses into the bottle. Repeat for the second bottle.

6 Carefully shave one end of the pieces of balsa wood with a craft knife until it fits snugly into the bottle. Repeat for the other bottle. An adult should do this stage.

7 Adults only should glue the balsa wood into the bottles with strong glue. When the strong glue is completely dry, a child can wind bright tape around the handles, and paint the ends of the handles. Leave the paint to dry completely before using the maracas.

Number Blocks

Turn adding, subtracting and dividing sums into a game with these chunky wooden cubes. They can also be piled on top of each other like building blocks. Store them in a box decorated to match. Children can help with the painting.

YOU WILL NEED
15 x 15 x 5cm (6 x 6 x 2in)
  piece of wood
pencil
ruler
saw
abrasive paper
emulsion (latex) or acrylic paint,
  in assorted shades
paintbrush
varnish and brush

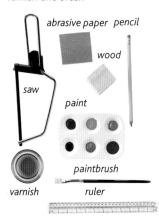

abrasive paper   pencil

wood

saw

paint

paintbrush

varnish   ruler

1 Divide the piece of wood into nine cubes, and an adult should cut them out with a saw. Smooth the surfaces and edges thoroughly with abrasive paper.

2 Paint the cubes, using a different shade for each side. Leave the paint to dry.

3 Paint numbers and mathematical signs on to the wooden cubes in contrasting bright shades. When the paint has completely dried, varnish the blocks.

4 Find or make a box that is a suitable size for storing the blocks. Paint to match, leave to dry, then varnish inside and out so that the paint doesn't chip.

Building Block House

This pretty house is made out of building blocks, so putting it together is like doing a jigsaw puzzle. Each time you build the house, you can move the windows around to give a different scheme. Children can help with the painting.

YOU WILL NEED
15 x 15 x 5cm (6 x 6 x 2in)
  piece of wood
pencil
ruler
saw
abrasive paper
emulsion (latex) or acrylic paint,
  in assorted shades
paintbrush
20 x 10cm (8 x 4in) piece of
  wood, for the roof
varnish and brush

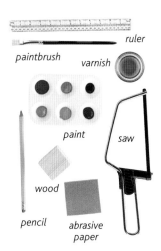

ruler

paintbrush

varnish

paint

saw

wood

pencil

abrasive paper

1 Divide the piece of wood into nine cubes, and an adult should cut them out with a saw. Smooth the surfaces and edges thoroughly with abrasive paper.

2 Paint the cubes, using a different shade for each side. Leave the paint to dry.

3 Take the piece of wood for the roof and saw off each side at a 45° angle. Sand the surface and corners thoroughly. Paint the roof, then, when dry, paint on the roof tiles.

4 Paint a door and windows on some of the cubes, then leave to dry completely. Varnish all the building blocks and the roof and leave to dry.

Dumper Truck

All sorts of heavy loads can be carried in this sturdy wooden truck. Adults must do the sawing and drilling.

YOU WILL NEED
65cm (26in) of 10 x 1cm
 (4 x ¹⁄₂in) pine
39.5cm (15¹⁄₂in) of 6 x 1cm
 (2¹⁄₂ x ¹⁄₂in) pine
ruler
pencil
saw
abrasive paper
PVA (white) glue and brush
60cm (24in) of 1 x 1cm
 (¹⁄₂ x ¹⁄₂in) pine lipping
drill, with 5mm (¹⁄₄in) and 4mm
 (³⁄₁₆in) drill bits
9.5cm (3³⁄₄in) of 5cm (2in)
 square pine
9cm (3¹⁄₂in) of 5cm (2in)
 triangle pine
23cm (9in) of 4mm- (³⁄₁₆in-)
 diameter dowel
10cm (4in) of 5cm- (2in-)
 diameter dowel
emulsion (latex) or acrylic paints
paintbrush
varnish and brush

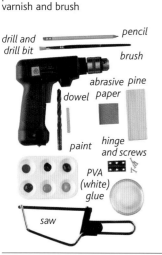

drill and *drill bit* · *pencil*
brush
abrasive · *pine*
dowel · *paper*
paint · *hinge and screws*
PVA (white) glue
saw

1 Adults only measure and cut two 29cm (11¹⁄₂in) lengths of 10 x 1cm (4 x ¹⁄₂in) pine. Cut the 6 x 1cm (2¹⁄₂ x ¹⁄₂in) pine into two pieces, 30cm (12in) and 9.5cm (3³⁄₄in). Sand all the edges with abrasive paper, until smooth. Glue together to make the back of the truck.

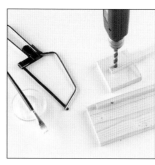

2 Cut the 1 x 1cm (¹⁄₂ x ¹⁄₂in) pine lipping in half using the saw. Holding the two pieces together as shown in the photograph, drill a 5mm (¹⁄₄in) hole in either end. Adults must do this stage. Glue to the underside of the remaining piece of 10 x 1cm (4 x ¹⁄₂in) pine. Leave to dry.

3 Glue the square and triangular pieces of wood together to make the cabin for the truck. Glue this to one end of the piece made in step 2. Attach the hinge to the back end of the truck base and to the bottom of the truck's storage section made in step 1.

4 Cut four 2.5cm (1in) lengths from the 5cm (2in) diameter dowel, for the wheels. Carefully drill a hole halfway through each length in the middle of the wheels. Cut the 4mm (³⁄₁₆in) dowel in half for the axles. Glue one end of each piece into the drilled holes in two of the wheels.

5 Paint the truck and the wheels. A child can help with this. When the paint is completely dry, apply a coat of varnish.

6 Assemble the wheels by pushing the 4mm (³⁄₁₆in) dowel through the two sets of holes under the truck. Glue the remaining two wheels on to either end.

Dog Jigsaw

It is easy to make your own large-scale jigsaw. A template for the dog is supplied but you could also make a jigsaw of your own pet, or choose a different shape. Children can help paint the design and stick on the self-adhesive fabric spots.

YOU WILL NEED
pencil
cardboard
craft (utility) knife
acrylic paint, in assorted shades
paintbrush
ruler
about 20 self-adhesive
 fabric spots
40 x 30cm (16 x 12in) piece of
 adhesive-backed felt
45 x 35cm (18 x 14in) piece of
 thick cardboard

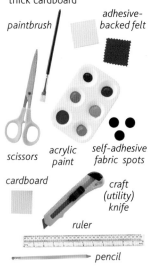

paintbrush

adhesive-backed felt

scissors

acrylic paint

self-adhesive fabric spots

cardboard

craft (utility) knife

ruler

pencil

1 Enlarge the template at the front of the book to 36cm (14in) long. Draw around the dog shape on to cardboard and an adult can carefully cut it out with a craft knife.

2 Paint the dog as illustrated, or using your own design. Children will love helping to paint the jigsaw. Leave the paint to dry.

3 Using a ruler, divide the dog into four or five simple pieces. An adult should then cut along the lines with the craft knife. Stick three or four self-adhesive fabric spots on the back of each piece.

4 Make the base by placing the thick card in the middle of the felt, then fold over the edges and stick them down securely.

Refrigerator Magnets

There are several modelling materials you could use in this project, including polymer clay. Whichever material you use, it is important to follow the instructions on the packet. Children can make these fun magnets, with supervision.

YOU WILL NEED
modelling medium
rolling pin (optional)
modelling tools (optional)
acrylic paints, in assorted shades
paintbrush
magnets
strong glue

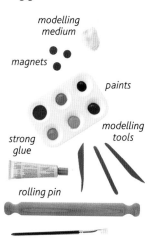

modelling medium

magnets

paints

strong glue

modelling tools

rolling pin

paintbrush

1 To make the teapot and the cups and saucers, shape each with your fingers, adding small pieces of the modelling medium for the details. If you are using polymer clay, you will need to roll it out first with a rolling pin and cut out the shapes with a modelling tool.

2 For the snail, roll out a length of modelling medium about 15cm (6in) long and coil it around to form the shape of a shell and body. Add on small pieces for the antennae.

3 Leave the shapes to harden, if necessary, then paint them in bright shades and leave to dry completely. If you are using polymer clay, you do not need to paint it.

4 Glue a magnet on to the back of each shape with strong glue. An adult must do this. Leave the glue to harden before placing the magnets on the refrigerator.

Squeaky Floor Cushion

Make a large, comfortable cushion for sitting or lying on the floor but watch out – this joke cushion has a squeaker hidden underneath each of the spots! The back is made in two pieces so that you can insert a cushion pad. Older children will be able to help make this, with supervision.

YOU WILL NEED
scraps of fabric
scissors
6 squeakers
needle and matching
  sewing threads
paper
pencil
felt, in 6 different shades
62cm (25in) square of plain
  fabric, for the front
2 pieces of fabric 62 x 40cm
  (25 x 16in), for the back
60cm (24in) square cushion pad

dressmaker's needle
squeaker
sewing thread
felt   fabric
pencil
scissors

1 Cut out twelve 6cm (2½in) squares of fabric. Stitch the squares together in pairs around three sides. Insert a squeaker inside each square, then stitch up the openings.

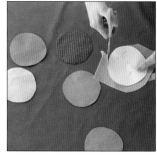

2 Draw around a mug or tumbler with pencil to make a round paper template. Place the paper template on the different pieces of felt and cut out six circles.

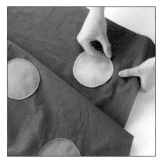

3 Arrange the felt circles on the square of plain fabric to make a nice design. Place a fabric-covered squeaker under each circle, then stitch around the edge.

4 Turn under a double hem along one long edge of each piece of fabric for the cushion back. Hand- or machine-stitch it in place.

5 With right sides facing, lay the two back pieces on top of the cushion front so that they overlap slightly. Hand- or machine-stitch around all four sides.

6 Turn the cushion cover right side out and insert the cushion pad.

Sunny Flower Blackboard

This novel blackboard should make sums and spelling more fun! Make it to fit your wall. If you have an electric jigsaw (saber saw), you can use it to cut out the flower shape, otherwise use a coping saw. Children can help paint.

YOU WILL NEED
MDF (medium-density
   fiberboard)
pencil
saw
abrasive paper
emulsion (latex) paint,
   in assorted shades
paintbrush
blackboard paint
bradawl or awl
2 screw eyes
string

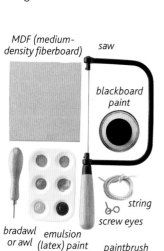

MDF (medium-density fiberboard)
saw
blackboard paint
string
screw eyes
bradawl or awl
emulsion (latex) paint
paintbrush
pencil
abrasive paper

1 Draw the flower on the wood and cut out using a saw. For the middle, use a pencil and string to draw a circle, as shown, or draw around a plate. Smooth the edges with abrasive paper.

2 Paint each petal a different shade, leave to dry, then paint a second coat. Leave to dry.

3 Paint the middle of the flower with two coats of blackboard paint. Leave to dry.

4 Turn the flower over. Mark two points, one on each side, and make small holes with a bradawl or awl. Screw the screw eyes into the holes until they are tight. Tie a piece of string securely to each screw eye, allowing some slack for hanging.

Village Play Mat

Children can help make this waterproof, hardwearing mat, which can be any size you like. Adhesive plastics are ideal for the stick-on shapes, but if these are not available use oil cloth, and an adult can glue it on with strong glue.

YOU WILL NEED
adhesive plastic or oil cloth,
  in assorted shades as well
  as black
scissors
large piece of oil cloth
strong glue and brush, optional
assorted toy cars, farm animals,
  people etc

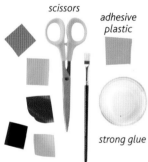

scissors

adhesive plastic

strong glue

oil cloth   *glue brush*

toys

1 Cut strips of black adhesive plastic or oil cloth for the roads and position these on the large piece of oil cloth. Stick the roads in place, using glue if necessary. Cut thin strips 4cm (1½in) long in grey or white, and stick down the middle of the roads.

2 Cut out green shapes from adhesive plastic or oil cloth for the trees and brown shapes for tree trunks. Stick small spots on some of the trees for apples.

3 Cut several squares and rectangles in different sizes for the various buildings – houses, a school, a hospital etc. Stick on door, window and roof shapes. Cut a round blue shape for the pond and stick bright fish shapes on top. Leave to dry.

4 Position all the cut-out shapes on the mat, then stick them in place, using glue and a brush if necessary. Add a few clumps of rushes around the edge of the pond and grass between the buildings. If you are using glue, leave it to dry.

Toy Garage

This is the perfect place to park toy cars at night, and to play with them during the day. Children can help with the painting.

YOU WILL NEED

1.2m x 50cm x 6mm
   (1¼yd x 20in x ¼in) birch
   plywood sheet
pencil
fretsaw or bandsaw
1.5m x 3.4cm x 8mm
   (1¾yd x 1⅓in x ⅜in) pine
60cm (24in) half-round beading
abrasive paper
wood glue and brush
masking tape
white undercoat
emulsion (latex) paint,
   in assorted shades
paintbrush

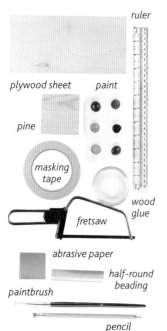

ruler
plywood sheet   *paint*
pine
masking tape
wood glue
fretsaw
abrasive paper
paintbrush
half-round beading
pencil

1 Trace the garage shapes from the template at the front of the book. Transfer them on to the plywood sheet and cut out. Cut the pine into one length of 39.5cm (15½in), one of 39.2cm (15⅜in) and two of 15cm (6in). Cut the half-round beading into six lengths of 10cm (4in). Tilt the bandsaw table to 45 degrees and cut an angle along the top and bottom of the ramp. Sand all the pieces with abrasive paper.

2 Glue the four wall sections on to the base of the garage, using masking tape to hold them in position while the glue dries completely. Make sure the walls are positioned so that they are straight and at right angles to each other. Make any adjustments before the glue dries.

3 Glue the six 10cm (4in) pieces of half-round beading to the uprights, to act as pillars that support the upper level of the garage. Once the glue securing the uprights in position has dried, carefully position the upper level on top of the columns and glue it in place. Leave the glue to dry completely.

4 Glue the plywood lengths around the roof. Place them against the facing edges of the roof, supported by the pillars.

5 Glue the car ramp neatly into position on the top and bottom levels of the toy garage. Leave the glue to dry completely.

6 Paint the garage with undercoat, then ask children to help paint on the details. Finally, varnish the garage and leave to dry.

DOLLS, PUPPETS AND SOFT TOYS

Playtime Stage

Dress up a cardboard box with bright paper, pretty fabric and paint and, hey presto, you have a theatre! Now all you need to do is make some characters to perform in it. Children will love helping to paint this simple project.

YOU WILL NEED
large cardboard box
pencil
ruler
craft (utility) knife
masking tape
paint
paintbrush
fabric, 50cm (20in) x the height
  of the box
scissors
PVA (white) glue and brush
bright paper, in 3 shades

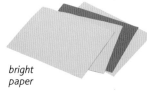

craft (utility) knife

PVA (white) glue

paint

fabric

masking tape

scissors

paintbrush

ruler

pencil

bright paper

1 Draw a rectangle on the top half of one side of the box and cut out, using a craft knife. Cut away the back of the box and half the base, leaving enough support to allow it to stand. An adult must do this. Strengthen the joins with masking tape.

2 Paint the inside of the box a bright shade. A child can help with this. Leave the paint to dry.

3 Cut the fabric in half to make two curtains 25cm (10in) wide. Fold the fabric into pleats along the top of each curtain and secure them by wrapping them with masking tape. Glue the curtains either side of the stage front.

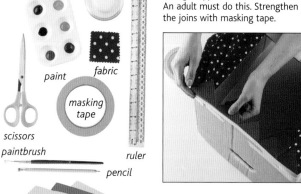

4 Cut a piece of paper the width of the stage and 10cm (4in) deep. Mark a line 2cm (¾in) from the edge and score with scissors so that it will fold. Cut a zigzag line along the bottom edge and glue to the theatre.

5 Measure the sides and top of the theatre using a ruler and cut out pieces of bright paper to fit. Let a child choose which shades are used. Glue the pieces of paper in place and leave to dry.

6 Cut wiggly strips of paper in a contrasting shade (a child could choose this). Glue these strips of paper on to the front of the stage and leave to dry completely before using the theatre.

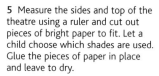

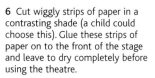

Finger Puppets

These two fairytale characters are easy to make and children of all ages can get involved. The princess puppet is made the same way as the frog. Be careful not to use too much glue and allow the glue to dry before sticking on the next shape.

YOU WILL NEED
paper
pencil
scissors
felt, in shades as illustrated
fabric glue and brush

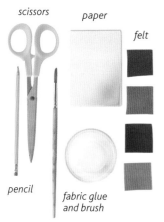

scissors

paper

felt

pencil

fabric glue and brush

1 Trace the princess and frog shapes from the templates at the front of the book on to paper. Cut the shapes out of felt, choosing a suitable shade for each piece. Children should be supervised when using scissors. Glue the two pieces for the base together, leaving the bottom edge open.

2 To make the frog finger puppet, glue the eyes and arms on to one side of the puppet, as shown in the photograph above.

3 Leave the glue to dry, then add the large mouth shape in the middle of the face. Leave to dry.

4 Finally add the details for the fingers, mouth and nostrils. Leave to dry completely before using.

Glove Puppets

An older child can have a go at making a simple glove puppet. Make ones for each hand, so they can perform together. If your child's hands are a different size to the template, simply draw around the hand and add a generous seam allowance.

YOU WILL NEED
pencil
paper
scissors
felt, blanket or wool fabric
embroidery thread (floss):
   blue and red
tapestry needle
knitting wool (yarn)
buttons

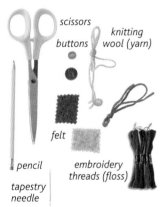

scissors
buttons
knitting wool (yarn)
felt
pencil
embroidery threads (floss)
tapestry needle

1 Trace the glove template from the front of the book on to paper and cut it out. Draw around the template on to the felt or fabric and cut out two glove shapes. Embroider blue eyes and a red mouth on one shape. Children should be supervised when using scissors and a needle.

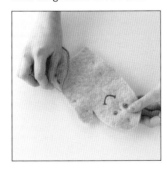

2 Place the two shapes together, wrong sides together, and sew around the edge in running stitch. Leave the bottom edge open so a hand can be inserted.

3 For the hair, stitch short lengths of knitting wool through the top of the glove and knot in place.

4 Finally stitch a row of buttons down the middle of the front. Ensure they are securely fastened.

Paper Fastener Puppet

It's amazing what you can do with basic equipment such as paper fasteners. Here they are used to joint the limbs of this smartly dressed puppet, so that you can make him wave and dance. An older child will be able to make this project.

YOU WILL NEED
thin card (stock)
pencil
scissors
paint, in assorted shades
paintbrush
4 paper fasteners
embroidery thread (floss)
electrical tape

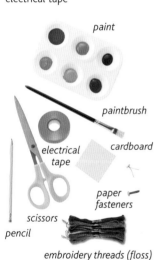

paint

paintbrush

electrical tape

cardboard

paper fasteners

scissors

pencil

embroidery threads (floss)

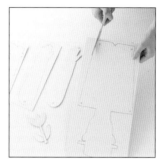

1 Trace the puppet templates from the front of the book. You will need two arms and two legs. Draw around the shapes on to thin card and cut out, using scissors. Adult supervision is required if a child uses scissors.

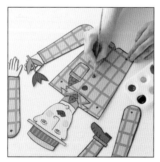

2 Paint the shapes in background shades and leave to dry, then paint the details of the man's checked suit and his face. Leave to dry.

3 Carefully make holes on the arms and legs, as shown on the templates. Make four holes on the body, as shown. Attach the limbs to the body with the paper fasteners.

4 Using electrical tape, stick a double length of embroidery thread behind the top of the puppet's head so that you can hang him up on a pinboard or wall.

Clay Doll

This doll is made in the traditional Mexican way, with the arms and legs tied to the body with threads. It is very fragile, so this toy may be best kept on a shelf as an ornament. Children can help shape and decorate this lovely doll.

YOU WILL NEED
self-hardening modelling clay
modelling tool
acrylic paint, in assorted shades
paintbrush
strong embroidery thread (floss)

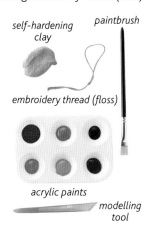

self-hardening clay   *paintbrush*

embroidery thread (floss)

acrylic paints

modelling tool

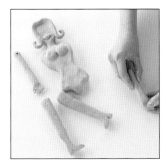

1 Shape the body, arms and legs out of the clay as shown in the photograph. Make sure the arms and legs are the same size. Lay the clay body pieces on a board or other flat surface.

2 Using a modelling tool, carefully pierce a hole at the top of each limb and at each corner of the body, as shown in the photograph. Leave the modelling clay to dry in a warm place overnight, or as directed in the packet instructions.

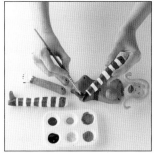

3 When the clay body pieces have fully hardened, paint them in bright shades as shown in the photograph, or devise your own design. Leave the paint to dry completely.

4 Tie the arms and legs to the body with lengths of embroidery thread, leaving enough slack for them to move freely. Tie bows to secure the threads in place.

Rag Doll

Little girls will love this calico doll. First make the doll, then make her an outfit to wear, such as a dress and pantaloons. This is quite a complex project, but an older child with some sewing experience will be able to help with some elements.

YOU WILL NEED
paper
pencil
scissors
50cm x 1m (20 x 39in) calico
matching sewing thread
dressmaker's needle
knitting needle, optional
scraps of felt: blue and pink
embroidery thread (floss):
  blue, pink and red
tapestry needle
yellow knitting wool (yarn)
ribbon

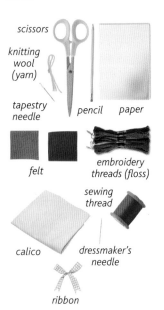

scissors

knitting
wool
(yarn)

tapestry
needle   pencil   paper

felt   embroidery
              threads (floss)

              sewing
              thread

calico   dressmaker's
              needle

ribbon

1 Trace the templates and cut out. Fold the calico in half and draw around the shapes. Cut the body shape out once and the arm and leg shapes twice. Stitch the shapes together in pairs, leaving an opening in each. Adult supervision is required.

2 Turn all the pieces right side out and fill the component parts with stuffing until firm. Use a knitting needle if necessary to push the stuffing into the furthest corners. Neatly slip-stitch the openings to close them securely.

3 Pinch the tops of the arms and legs, then stitch though all the layers to retain the pleat.

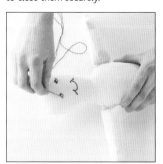

4 Stitch the arms and legs securely to the body as shown above. If a child does this, then an adult should check that the limbs are properly attached and that the doll will withstand use.

5 Cut two small circles out of blue felt for the doll's eyes, and two slightly larger circles out of pink felt for her cheeks. Stitch on to the face, using embroidery threads. Embroider the mouth in red in running stitch.

6 Stitch short lengths of yellow wool through the top of the doll's head, tying each in a knot close to the head. Then give the hair a neat trim. Tie the ribbon in a bow and stitch in position as shown.

Rag Doll's Dress

The dress is decorated with a double felt collar and ribbon roses. It fastens at the back so a child can practise dressing and undressing the doll. Older children with some sewing experience can attempt this project, with help.

YOU WILL NEED
paper
pencil
scissors
50cm x 1m (20 x 39in) dress fabric
matching sewing thread
dressmaker's needle
felt, in a contrasting shade
ribbon roses
poppers (snap fasteners)

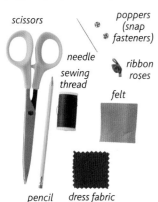

scissors

poppers (snap fasteners)

needle

ribbon roses

sewing thread

felt

pencil   dress fabric

1 Trace the dress templates from the front of the book on to paper. Fold the fabric in half, place the pattern piece for the front on the fold and cut out. Cut two sleeves and two back pieces. Stitch the sleeve seams and hem the cuffs. Leave 6mm (¼in) seam allowance. Adult supervision is required.

2 Stitch the two back pieces to the front piece, right sides together. Turn under 6mm (¼in) and hem neatly using slip stitch.

3 Right sides together, stitch the shoulder seams. Turn the dress right side out. Place the sleeves through the armholes as shown and tack (baste) in position, then stitch neatly in position.

4 Turn over 6mm (¼in) around the neck edge to the right side and stitch. Trace the collar template on to paper and cut out twice from felt. Stitch both collars around the neck edge. Decorate the dress with ribbon roses. Turn the raw edges of the back opening under 2cm (¾in) to the wrong side and stitch. Stitch poppers to either side of the opening.

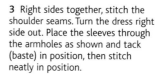

Rag Doll's Pantaloons and Boots

Make the pantaloons in fabric that contrasts with the rag doll's dress. Her boots are made from scraps of fabric.

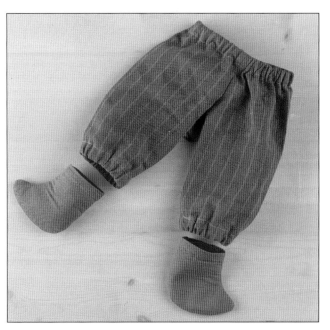

YOU WILL NEED
paper
pencil
scissors
scrap of fabric for the boots
matching sewing threads
dressmaker's needle
70cm (27½in) x 1m (39in) dress fabric for the pantaloons
60cm (24in) narrow elastic
safety pin

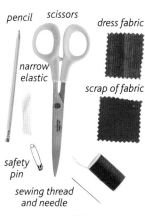

pencil scissors dress fabric

narrow elastic

scrap of fabric

safety pin

sewing thread and needle

1 Trace the boot template on to paper. Fold a small piece of fabric in half, draw around the shape twice and cut out. Stitch two boot shapes together, right sides facing, leaving the top open. Repeat for the other boot. Adult supervision is required.

2 Trace the pantaloons template. Fold the fabric in half, right sides facing, then place the pattern on the fold as marked. Cut out twice. Keeping the fabric folded in half, stitch along the inside leg.

3 Turn one pantaloon leg right side out and place inside the other leg, with raw edges matching along the crotch seam. Stitch the crotch seam and turn right side out. Fold the waist edge over 3cm (1¼in) to the wrong side, then stitch around the waist 1cm (½in) from the top, leaving a small opening. Repeat at the bottom of each leg.

4 Cut the elastic into three lengths: one measuring 30cm (12in) and two measuring 15cm (6in). Pin a safety pin to one end of the long piece and thread it through the waistband. Pull both ends to gather the waist and stitch firmly together. Repeat for the pantaloon legs. Check all the seams are securely sewn, then dress the doll.

Doll's House

This little house is ready to furnish and decorate. The whole front is attached with a hinge so that you can open it and see inside. Instead of buying expensive doll's house furniture, make your own using matchboxes and cardboard. Children can help with the painting and some sticking.

YOU WILL NEED
1.8m x 37cm (2⅛yd x 15in) of 6mm (¼in) birch plywood sheet
4 x 2.2cm (1½ x ⅞in) pine
pencil
bandsaw
drill
fretsaw
abrasive paper
wood glue and brush
masking tape
3cm (1¼in) of 12mm (⁹⁄₁₆in) diameter dowel
white emulsion (latex) paint, as undercoat
emulsion (latex) paint, in pastel shades
2 brass hinges
screws

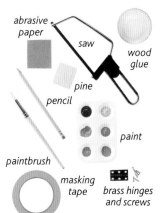

abrasive paper
saw
wood glue
pine
pencil
paint
paintbrush
masking tape
brass hinges and screws

1 Cut out the templates from the plywood. Tilt the bandsaw table to 45° and cut either side of the roof panels and the top of each side wall at an angle. An adult must do this.

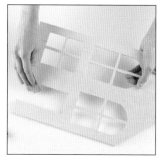

2 Trace details from the template on to the front of the house. Drill a hole through each separate area and cut out the windows and door using a fretsaw. Sand any rough edges.

3 Glue the interior wall and upper floor together at right angles. Glue the back wall and side walls to the base. Use tape to hold the pieces in position while the glue dries.

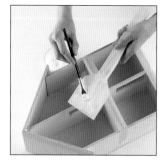

4 Glue the interior fittings and the roof support carefully in place, then glue the roof panels in position. Glue the chimney stack to the roof by an outside wall. Leave the glue to dry completely.

5 Drill a large hole through the top board of the chimney and fit the dowel into it. Glue the chimney to the top of the chimney stack. Position and then stick the door, windowsills and gable to the front.

6 Paint the house with white emulsion paint as an undercoat. When dry, paint on details in bright paints. Finish with varnish. Attach the front to the main part of the house, with the hinges and screws.

Doll's House Furniture

Children will love helping to make doll's house furniture using matchboxes, corks, bottle tops and other odds and ends.

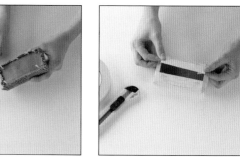

YOU WILL NEED
scissors
masking tape
PVA (white) glue
felt
stuffing
embroidery thread (floss)
dressmaker's needle
7 small matchboxes
bright paper
matches
lampshade fringing
large matchbox
craft (utility) knife
emulsion (latex) or acrylic paint
paintbrush
6 paper fasteners
2 plastic bottle tops
2 corks
buttons

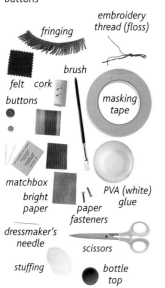

fringing
embroidery thread (floss)
brush
felt *cork*
buttons
masking tape
matchbox
bright paper
PVA (white) glue
paper fasteners
dressmaker's needle
scissors
stuffing
bottle top

1 CUSHIONS: For each cushion, cut two 4cm (1½in) squares of felt. Trap a small amount of stuffing between them, then stitch around the edge, using embroidery thread. Stitch a button on each side. Older children may be able to do this, with supervision and some help.

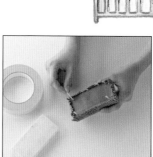

2 BED: Fasten three matchboxes together in a row with masking tape. Cover with bright paper. Pierce a hole in each corner underneath the bed and place a match without a head in each hole. Cut a length of fringing to fit around the bed and glue in place.

3 WARDROBE: Cut two holes for doors in the front of a large matchbox and reinforce the holes with masking tape.

4 Cover the wardrobe doors with pieces of bright paper, then paint the rest of the box in a contrasting shade. Insert a paper fastener through each door to look like a handle. Glue the bottle tops on the bottom of the wardrobe and leave to dry completely.

5 CHEST OF DRAWERS (BUREAU): Neatly line up four small matchboxes, then stick them together with masking tape.

6 Glue a piece of bright paper over the chest-of-drawers, then paint the drawers. When the paint is dry, pierce a paper fastener through the middle of each drawer. Cut the corks in half and paint. Once completely dry, glue the painted corks to the bottom.

More Ideas For Your Doll's House

Here are some more fixtures and fittings for your doll's house. The table, chair and staircase are all made out of folded card and the crockery is made out of polymer clay. Make as many chairs, cups and saucers as you like. Children can help to make most of the items.

YOU WILL NEED
bright thin card (stock)
pencils
craft (utility) knife
scissors
crayons
PVA (white) glue and brush
polymer clay
modelling tools
ruler

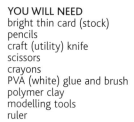

polymer clay

thin card (stock)

brush

pencil crayons

craft (utility) knife

PVA (white) glue

ruler

scissors

modelling tools

1 Trace the furniture shapes from the templates at the front of the book and transfer them on to thin card. Cut out, using a craft knife. Score along the fold lines with scissors. An adult should do this.

2 Shade in the shapes with bright crayons. These are most effective if you build up layers of different shades. Children can help do this.

3 Fold the furniture neatly along the fold lines. Check that everything lines up correctly, then glue the pieces in position. Children may require some help to do this.

4 For the staircase, fold a length of card into a concertina, with flaps on alternate stairs, and glue into place.

5 To make a saucer, flatten a small ball of polymer clay and decorate. Bake as directed on the packet.

6 To make a cup, make a hole in the middle of a small ball of polymer clay and add a small handle.

Fabric Dice

This larger-than-life dice will be useful for many games, and is a great way for children to learn about numbers. If you make two or three dice, they can be used to practise juggling Older children can do this project; younger ones can help with the gluing and choosing the fabric.

YOU WILL NEED
paper
pencil
ruler
assorted fabrics
scissors
sewing thread
dressmaker's needle
stuffing
felt, in assorted shades
fabric glue and brush

brush
fabric
sewing thread and needle
felt
stuffing
fabric glue
scissors
pencil
ruler

1 Make a paper template measuring 12cm (4¾in) square. Use to cut out six squares of fabric, in different shades. Allow an extra 6mm (¼in) seam allowance all around. Adult supervision is required.

2 With right sides together, stitch two squares along one side, leaving a 6mm (¼in) seam. Repeat with the other squares, joining them together to make a 'T' shape, as shown in the photograph above.

3 With right sides together, neatly slip-stitch the squares together to form a cube, leaving one side open. Turn the cube right side out, pushing out the corners so they are sharp and precise.

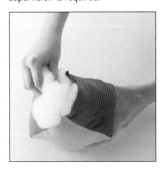

4 Fill the cube with stuffing until it is firm, but do not overstuff it or it will be hard to sew shut. Young children will enjoy helping with this. Stitch the opening closed securely using slip stitch.

5 Cut out circles of felt, in different shades that contrast with the fabric upon which they will be glued. You will need one of one shade, two of another, three of another, and so on until you finish with six spots.

6 Glue the felt circles on to the sides of the dice, arranging them as on a real dice. Look at a dice if you are unsure of the configuration. Leave the glue to dry completely before giving the dice to a child.

Character Skittles

Plastic bottles make excellent skittles, especially if you paint them to look like people. You can play the game indoors as well as outside if you use a soft ball. Children can do most of the steps in this project.

YOU WILL NEED
clean, empty plastic bottles
fretsaw
newspaper
PVA (white) glue and brush
water
paper baubles
strong glue
acrylic paint, in assorted shades
paintbrush
ribbon, in assorted shades

strong glue

newspaper

brush

paper bauble

PVA (white) glue

ribbon

paint

plastic bottle

fretsaw

1 Remove the labels from the bottles by soaking them in water. Saw off the top of each bottle as shown. An adult must do this.

2 Cover the bottles in papier-mâché (see Basic Techniques) and leave to dry completely. Children can help do this.

3 Glue a paper bauble on top of each bottle, using strong glue. An adult must do this; children should not use strong glue.

4 Paint the bottles and the bauble faces with a base coat. Leave the paint to dry.

5 Give each skittle a different character by painting on bright hair and clothes. Leave the second coat of paint to dry.

6 Tie a different piece of ribbon in a bow around the neck of each skittle.

Jumbo Dominoes

This is a giant, bright version of a fun game that children will love painting and then playing with. Make as many dominoes as you like – a traditional set has 28 pieces, but you will probably only need half that number.

YOU WILL NEED
pine plank wood
ruler
pencil
saw
abrasive paper
paint, in assorted shades
paintbrush
black adhesive spots
varnish and brush

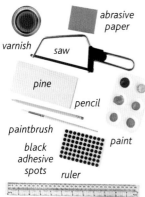

varnish
abrasive paper
saw
pine
pencil
paintbrush
black adhesive spots
paint
ruler

1 Measure 15 x 7.5cm (6 x 3in) rectangles on the wood and cut out using the fretsaw. Sand the surfaces and corners with abrasive paper.

2 Divide each rectangle in half to make two squares. Paint each half a different shade, leaving the paint to dry after painting the first before starting to paint the second.

3 Stick black spots on each face of the dominoes. Vary the number of spots from zero to six.

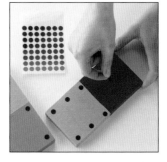

4 Finally, seal the dominoes by painting them with a layer of varnish, using a brush.

Star Draughts (Checkers)

Children can help paint the draughts board and make the matching draughts. Play the game in the same way as you would traditional draughts. This game is not suitable for young children, who may put the pieces in their mouths.

YOU WILL NEED
52 x 52cm (20 x 20in) MDF
  (medium-density fiberboard)
metal ruler
pencil
emulsion (latex) or acrylic paint,
  in 2 contrasting shades
paintbrush
masking tape, optional
varnish and brush
polymer clay, in 2 shades
  to match the board
small star cookie cutter

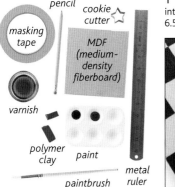

1 Using a ruler, divide the wood into 64 squares, each measuring 6.5 x 6.5cm (2½ x 2½in).

2 Paint alternate squares in the first shade. To help paint straight lines, you can mark out the squares with masking tape and remove it when the paint is dry.

3 Paint the remaining squares with the second shade. When the paint is dry, apply a coat of varnish.

4 For the draughts, roll the polymer clay to a thickness of about 5mm (or ¼in) thick. Using the cookie cutter, cut out twelve shapes from each shade. Bake, following the manufacturer's instructions, and allow to cool.

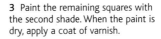

Felt Noughts and Crosses (Tic-tac-toe)

This game is ideal for journeys. The felt shapes are attached to the board with self-adhesive fabric so they can't move or fall off. Older children can make this project with supervision and younger ones can help position the shapes.

YOU WILL NEED

30 x 30cm (12 x 12in) thick cardboard
2 squares of adhesive felt, 32 x 32cm (13 x 13in) and 30 x 30cm (12 x 12in)
adhesive felt, in 3 contrasting shades
pencil
ruler
scissors
thin card (stock)
9 self-adhesive fabric spots
fabric glue and brush

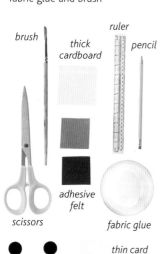

brush
thick cardboard
ruler
pencil
adhesive felt
scissors
fabric glue
thin card (stock)
self-adhesive fabric spots

1 Position the 32cm (13 in) square of felt centrally on the cardboard. Stick down, folding the edges over to the back.

2 Stick the 30cm (12in) square of adhesive felt so that it covers the back of the cardboard, making sure it is aligned before smoothing it down.

3 Cut four narrow strips of felt 1 x 32cm (¾ x 13in) in contrasting shades. Stick them across the board to make nine equal squares.

4 Trace the templates for the game pieces on to card and cut out. Cover each shape with felt on both sides. You will need four of each shape, using a different shade for the noughts (Os) and the crosses (Xs).

5 Cut out the felt shapes, leaving the card inside.

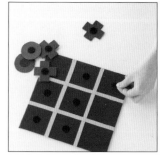

6 Glue the furry side of the self-adhesive fabric spots on to the middle of the noughts and crosses. Glue the looped side in the middle of the squares on the board. Leave to dry before playing the game.

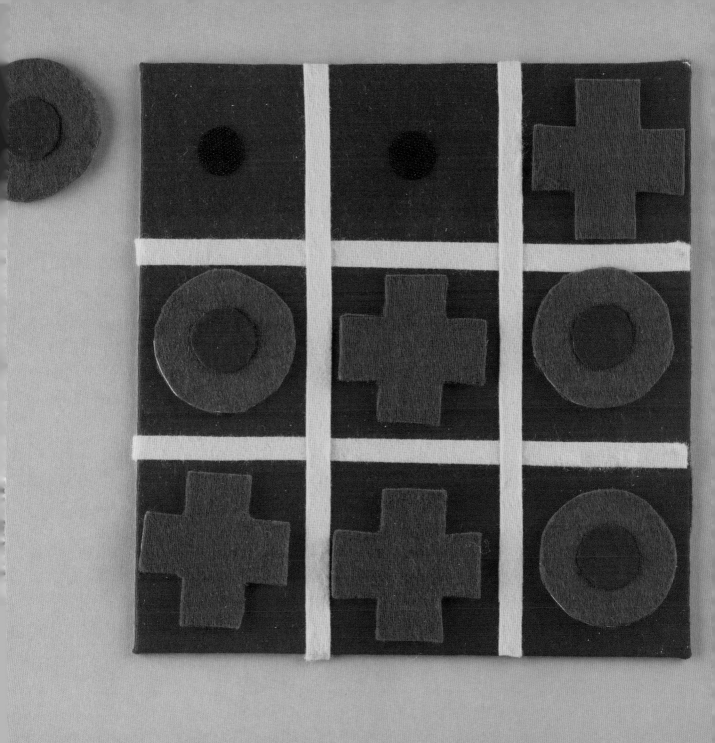

Teacup Basketball

This indoor basketball game will certainly cheer up a rainy day, both when making it with children and then playing it. The balls used here are small pompoms but you can also use balls of crumpled paper or table tennis balls.

YOU WILL NEED
pencil
paper
scissors
35 x 60cm (13¾ x 24in) thin card (stock)
paint, in assorted shades
paintbrush
bradawl or awl
single-hole punch
thin cord or string
5 pipe cleaners in different shades
electrical tape
pompoms

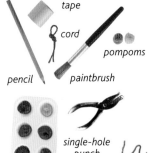

thin card (stock)

bradawl or awl

scissors

electrical tape

cord

pompoms

pencil   paintbrush

single-hole punch

paint   pipe cleaner

1 Trace the teacup template from the front of the book on to paper. Draw around it on to the card five times. Position the shapes as shown in the main photograph.

2 Paint the background, outlining the teacup shapes. When the paint is dry, paint the cups in different patterns. Leave to dry, then paint a number (1–5) on each cup.

3 Using a bradawl or awl, pierce a hole on either side of the rim of each cup. Punch a hole in the top corners of the card and thread through cord or string for hanging.

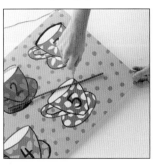

4 Thread a pipe cleaner through the holes on each cup.

5 On the back of the cardboard, coil the ends of the pipe cleaners and flatten them so they lie flat.

6 Stick pieces of tape over the ends of the pipe cleaners to secure. Turn the card over and shape the pipe cleaners so that they stick out in semicircle basket shapes.

Pyramid Game

This game is best made by adults, although children can help paint it. The object is to move the whole pyramid from one end of the board to the other, moving only one piece at a time and never placing a larger square on a smaller square.

YOU WILL NEED
30 x 30cm (12 x 12in) of 6mm
 (¼in) birch plywood sheet
saw
abrasive paper
pencil
drill and 8mm (⅜in) bit
15cm (6in) of 8mm (⅜in)
 diameter dowel
PVA (white) glue and brush
water-based ink, in 5 shades
paintbrush

drill and drill bit

saw

1 Cut a 10cm- (4in-) wide strip from the plywood and sand the edges. Draw a line along the middle, then mark points 5cm (2in), 15cm (6in) and 25cm (10in) from one end. Drill holes at these points.

water-based ink

plywood sheet

dowel

paintbrush

pencil

abrasive paper

PVA (white) glue

2 Cut the dowel into three equal lengths and sand the ends. Glue into the holes in the plywood.

3 Cut squares from the remaining plywood in graduating sizes: 8cm (3in), 7cm (2¾in), 6cm (2½in), 5cm (2in) and 4cm (1½in). Find the middle of each and drill a hole.

4 Stain the squares different shades, using water-based ink.

Magnetic Fish

See how many goldfish you can catch – the highest score wins the game. To make a fishing rod, tie a piece of bright string to the magnet. Tie the other end to a garden stick or cane. Children can make this game, with supervision.

YOU WILL NEED
paper
pencil
thin card (stock)
scissors
paint, in assorted shades
paintbrush
bright metal paper clips
  (fasteners)
shallow box
magnet

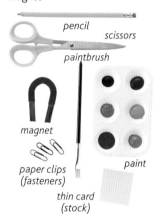

pencil

scissors

paintbrush

magnet

paper clips
(fasteners)

paint

thin card
(stock)

1 Trace the fish template on to paper. Draw around the shape five or six times on card and carefully cut out with scissors.

2 Paint the fish. Leave them to dry, then paint a different number on each one.

3 Attach a paper clip to the mouth of each fish.

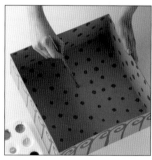

4 Paint the box blue and leave it to dry. Using a darker shade, paint wavy lines around the edge to represent water. Leave to dry completely before using.

Paper Windmill

This windmill spins around in a breeze, but remember it is made of paper so do not leave it outdoors in the rain. An adult must do the drilling and attach the windmill to the stick.

YOU WILL NEED
bright paper, in 3 shades
scissors
PVA (white) glue and brush
ruler
pencil
paper clip (fastener)
darning needle, optional
25cm (10in) length of dowel
abrasive paper
drill
cork

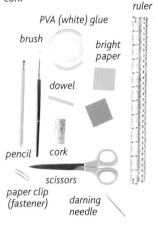

PVA (white) glue
brush
bright paper
ruler
dowel
pencil
cork
scissors
paper clip (fastener)
darning needle

drill and drill bit
abrasive paper

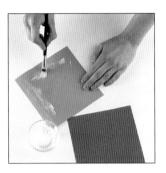

1 Cut out two 15cm (6in) squares from paper, each in a different shade. Glue them together.

2 Using a pencil, draw a diagonal line across the middle of the square in both directions. Measure 7cm (2¾in) from each corner and mark with a dot. Cut up to the dots. Erase the pencil lines.

3 Gently bend every other point into the middle of the square as shown in the photograph above. Glue together the corners, holding the paper in place until the glue dries and they are secure.

4 Cut out a small circle from the third shade of paper. Straighten out a paper clip, bend one end into a coil and glue on to the middle of the circle.

5 Gently push the other end of the paper clip through the middle of the windmill, making a hole with a needle first if necessary. Sand the ends of the dowel with abrasive paper, then carefully drill a hole 3cm (1½in) from one end, resting the dowel on a piece of wood.

6 Push the sharp end of the paper clip through the hole in the end of the dowel. Glue the end of the paper clip and push it into a piece of cork for safety.

Skipping Rope (Jump Rope)

The simplest toys provide the most fun, and children can play skipping games for hours. Adjust the length of the rope to suit the child's height.

YOU WILL NEED
34cm (13½in) plastic tubing
craft (utility) knife
abrasive paper
about 2m (2¼yd) smooth rope
lighter

smooth rope

plastic tubing

craft (utility) knife

abrasive paper

1 Cut the plastic tubing in half, using a craft knife. Adults only should do this. Smooth the edges with abrasive paper.

2 Thread each end of the rope through the tube.

3 Ask the child to check the length of the rope by skipping with it, then knot the ends securely at the required length.

4 Burn the ends of the rope to prevent them from fraying. Adults only must do this and great care should be taken.

Mini Pinball

This is a real game of skill and chance. Each player rolls a marble along the tilted board, dodging the players on the field to try and reach one of the goals. The smaller the hole, the higher the score! An adult should make the majority of this project, although children can help paint it.

YOU WILL NEED
70 x 40cm (27½ x 16in) of
   12mm (⁹⁄₁₆in) thick MDF
   (medium-density fiberboard)
ruler
pencil
coping saw
abrasive paper
1.6m (1⅔yd) of 1 x 1cm
   (½ x ½in) wooden lipping
PVA (white) glue
drill
60cm (24in) of 8mm (⁵⁄₁₆in)
   diameter dowel
paint, in assorted shades
paintbrush
marbles

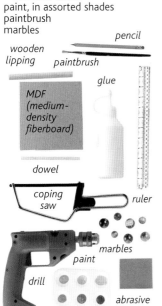

wooden lipping
pencil
paintbrush
glue
MDF (medium-density fiberboard)
dowel
ruler
coping saw
marbles
paint
drill
abrasive paper

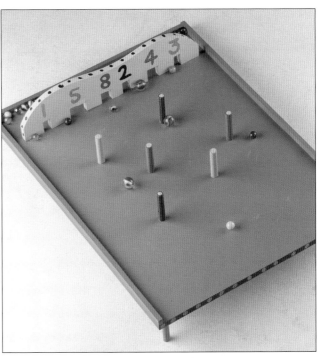

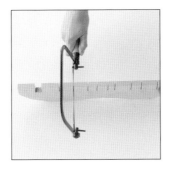

1 Cut a 10cm (4in) strip off the short side of the wood, then cut 5cm (2in) off one end. Using a saw, cut out holes of different sizes along one long edge. Sand the edges.

2 Cut the lipping into two 60cm (24in) strips and one 38cm (15in) strip. Glue around the edge of the remaining piece of MDF. Drill six holes at random on one side of the board. On the other, drill a hole in each corner of one of the short sides.

3 Cut the dowel into eight equal lengths. Glue one into each hole, including the two supports at the back of the board. Glue the other piece of MDF upright near the end of the board, allowing space on either side for the marbles to pass.

4 Paint the pinball table and leave to dry. Paint score numbers above each hole – the smaller the hole, the greater the number.

Big Foot Stilts

Children will love walking about on these bright giant feet!
If possible, ask the child for whom the stilts are intended to
stand on the cans so that you can measure the length of rope
needed. They can help stick on the stars at the end.

YOU WILL NEED
2 large, empty cans,
  the same size
softened non-hardening
  modelling clay
bradawl or awl
spray paint
enamel paint, in contrasting shade
paintbrush
adhesive stars
rope, see above for measurement

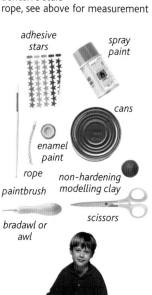

adhesive
stars

spray
paint

cans

enamel
paint

rope

non-hardening
modelling clay

paintbrush

scissors

bradawl or
awl

1 Remove the labels from the cans.
Place a ball of softened modelling
clay on either side of the top of
each can. Pierce a hole through the
modelling clay with a bradawl or
awl, then remove the modelling clay.

2 Place the cans on a well-protected
surface, preferably outdoors. Spray
with spray paint and leave to dry.
Spray on a second coat if necessary.

3 Paint the top of the cans with
enamel paint. Leave to dry.

4 Decorate the cans with adhesive
stars; children can help with this.

5 Ask the child to stand on the
cans. Measure the length of rope
needed, then thread one piece of
rope through the holes on each
can. Tie the ends in a knot.

6 Burn the ends of rope to prevent
them from fraying. An adult should
do this with care.

Soaring Kite

Take this kite out on a windy day and any child will be happy for hours. Choose a bright shade for the tail, to contrast with the kite and show up against the sky.

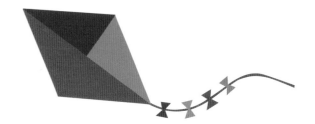

YOU WILL NEED

50 x 70cm (20 x 27½in) lightweight fabric
ruler
pencil
scissors
sewing thread
dressmaker's needle
65cm (26in) thin, strong nylon thread
small piece of contrast fabric, for the tail
2 pieces of 5mm (³⁄₁₆in) dowel, 68cm (26¾in) and 48cm (19in) long

scissors

fabric

sewing thread

dressmaker's needle

pencil

ruler

dowel

1 Fold the fabric in half lengthways. On the raw edges, mark 25cm (10in) down from the top. Cut from the fold point at each end to this mark. Open out the kite shape, fold over, place the cut edges together and stitch the seam.

2 Stitch the nylon thread securely to the two corners on either side of the kite.

3 Fold in each corner about 1cm (½in). Secure with two tacking (basting) stitches about 1cm (½in) apart, to go either side of the dowel.

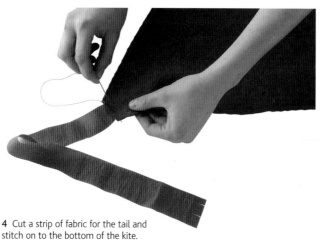

4 Cut a strip of fabric for the tail and stitch on to the bottom of the kite.

5 Lay the two pieces of dowel across the kite in an 'X' shape and insert the ends into the pockets made by the tacking stitches.

INDEX